MW00878354

CONTENTS

Appalachian Cryptids & Monsters

Justin H. Guess

INTRODUCTION

A cryptid is a creature whose existence hasn't been proven, and the study of this field of research is called cryptozoology. In the past, these creatures were called monsters or "boogers" all along the Appalachian Mountains, that run through Alabama, Georgia, Kentucky, Maryland, Mississippi, New York, North Carolina, Ohio, Pennsylvania, South Carolina, Tennessee, Virginia, and West Virginia. It's home to many strange beasts, and in this book, you'll read about the more famous ones, as well as those seldom mentioned.

This book doesn't include mythical creatures, fearsome critters, urban legends, cryptids created to sell books or push creationist narratives, legendary or mythological beasts, folkloric creatures, ghosts or spiritual beings, obvious hoaxes, or seek to interpret Indigenous tales.

BESSIE

Explored in Bill J. Shortridge's 2021 book, *Lake Erie Sea Monster*, the lake monster is described today as a plesiosaurus between 30 and 40 feet long with a grayish coloring.

It was first sighted in 1793 when the captain of the sloop, the Felicity, was out shooting ducks and spotted a serpent-like creature "more than a rod in length".

Reprinted from the Albany Argus, the September 19, 1817 edition of the *Alexandria Gazette & Daily Advertiser* documented that:

> *Independent of other corroborating statements, Mr. Watson, who is represented as a man of veracity, sates, that he has seen the lake serpent repeatedly, and fired several balls at him, at the distance of 20 rods, without the least apparent effect. He describes him as about 60 feet long, of a copper [color], with brilliant eyes, four inches in diameter. He has seen him in a coil, and extended upon the water.*

A similar sighting was documented in the July 25, 1861 edition of *The Highland Weekly News*, documenting that a "party of Dunkirk fishermen are ready to make an oath to the visual inspection of a sea serpent in Lake Erie, 'some sixteen feet in length, with head and tail erect, of a greenish color, and very action in its motions'".

A Detroit Post and Tribune entry was reprinted in the October 11, 1878 edition of the *Chicago Daily Tribune* documented another sighting:

And now comes another wild, dime-novel story about a sea-serpent, seen on Lake Erie. The captain of the [schooner] J. E. Baily, which arrived up yesterday, reports that when off Kettle Point, Lake Erie, he saw in the water ahead of his vessel a snake, which appeared to be not less than ten feet long, and from seven to ten inches around it. When seen its head was about two feet above the water, and a most ferocious head it was. Its fangs were immense. "The body was striped with black."

The July 25, 1891 The Indianapolis Journal article, *Jay County's Fifty-foot Snake*, recounts the experience of a group of people, saying:

The great serpent that was seen by the Lake Erie & Western [road master], a few days since, has again put in an appearance. It was seen this time by a band of [Romani persons] camped on Brooke's [Creek]. The story of the encounter is told as follows by the [Romani persons]: "We were on our way from Waukon, IA, to Dayton [OH], and camped last night on the banks of a small stream. We went to bed about [9:00 PM]. About midnight I was awakened by the barking of the dogs southeast of the camp, and soon after the horses broke their tethers and rushed away. By this time all the camp were on their feet, not knowing the cause of the trouble. In a moment there was a rushing sound and we saw the head of a monster snake coming rapidly toward us. Before we could collect our senses it was within ten feet of one of the children. My wife then snatched a brand from the smoldering campfire and struck it with all her might.

"The serpent reared its head at least [20] feet in the air and turning, in a second was gone. I never saw such a snake before. Its head was nine or ten inches broad and it must have been [50] feet in length. We stood for an hour after it was gone, afraid to move, and then built several fires around the camp to prevent its return. Out horses were scattered all over the country and could not be induced to return to the camp, so we had to hire a farmer to draw us to the pike."

This snake has been in the vicinity mentioned for the last six or seven years and the numbers of hogs and sheep that have disappeared are supposed to have become its prey.

In 1892, there was a flurry of sightings, many of which were documented in local newspapers. The first was in the May 21 Daily Tobacco Leaf-Chronicle article, *The Season is Now Open*, saying:

Two fishermen near Oak Harbor, [Ohio], declare they saw a veritable sea serpent in Lake Erie Monday evening, May 16. It was seen at two different times, and is described as about [25] feet long and a foot and a half in diameter in the thickest part of the body. Its head was large and flat, and there appeared to be several large fins, or flippers, and about five feet from the head. In was black in color, mottled with brown spots.

The July 16 The Evening World article, *Capt. Woods Reports One of Terrible Aspect and Fiery Eyes*, documents another sighting, saying:

The great sea serpent has begun his midsummer series of star performances, but this season ha has transferred the scene of his activity from the Atlantic coast to the Great Lakes. His first appearance in this location has created a sensation.

Early Wednesday morning, while the schooner Madeline Dowing, on its way from Buffalo to [Toledo, Ohio], was passing the Dunning, about [150] miles east of here in Lake Erie, [captain] Patrick Woods saw, about half a mile ahead, the waters of the lake lashed into a foam.

Drawing near, to the surprise of the captain and all on board, a huge sea serpent was seen thrashing and squirming about in the waters as if fighting with an unseen enemy. It soon quieted down and lay at full length on the surface of the lake.

[Captain] Woods estimates that it was about [50] feet in length and not less than four feet in circumference. Its head was projecting from the water about four feet. He says it was a terrible looking object. It had viciously sparkling, red eyes and a large head. Large fins were plainly seen. The body was dark brown in color.

As the vessel passed on its course, the snake was seen disporting itself on the lake. At the time he saw it in the lake was clam, and there could have been no mistake, he says, in recognizing the object.

The August 21 Los Angeles Herald article, *Bigger than Saucers*, documents another sighting, saying:

The sea serpent reported as appearing in Lake Erie off Sodus Point was seen again yesterday by Superintendent Mead and a number of officials of the Northern Central Railroad who left Sodus Point in the steam yacht Camelia for a fishing trip. When a short distance off from Spring's Bluff, captain Buys, who was standing in the front part of the boat leaning over the starboard rail, felt the roll of the boat as if from the swish of a dead sea. A sudden lurch caused him to look seaward, when he noticed a huge animal moving the same direction as the tug at a speed of about half as fast as the steamer was going.

He rang the engineer slowly up, so that he could get a better view of the monster, when it suddenly dived into the water, which was between [40] and [50] fathoms deep. The captain saw nothing else of the monster until he reached the point that evening. Between [5:00 and 6:00 PM] a party of excursionists who had been spending the day on Eagle Island, in the bay, noticed something floating off toward the bar that separates the lake from the bay, which looked like a huge log, only it seemed to be moving directly against the wind, and was heading toward the lake bluff. Filled [with] curiosity, and thinking that it might be the sea serpent, they got a row-boat and started over toward Leroy's Island, so as to reach the point and observe the animal's reaction. When the monster reached a shallow spot, directly in the course of the steamer Leroy, opposite the bluff on the island, where a large number of rushes were growing, it began to flounder around in the water, as if in pursuit of fish. The animal about the head resembled a horse, and about the body an African crocodile. Its teeth were in the lower jaw, and show that it was something akin to the shark. Dan Klung claims that he had the best view of the monster, as it was looking straight at him while he was observing it through the glass. He says its eyes appeared to be larger than saucers and slightly oblique.

The November 8 The Scranton Tribune article, *Lake Erie's Sea Serpent*, documents another close sighting of the cryptid, saying:

William Myrtle, a well known citizen of Monroe, [Michigan], north of [Toledo, Ohio], claims to have seen Lake Erie's famous sea serpent yesterday while fishing on the Rasin [River]. He says he saw what seemed to be a pug dog swimming toward him and he raised an oar as if to strike it.

Immediately the serpent reared its head fully four feet out of the water, showing a neck that resembled that of a giraffe. Some distance from the head were fins that were almost large enough for wings and still further down the body were short stumpy legs. Myrtle struck at it with an oar, whereupon it dived to the bottom of the river. The animal is exactly like the one described by a French fisherman, as having been seen at the mouth of Pelton Creek some years ago, and also like the serpent seen by the lake captain at the mouth of Portage [River], at Port Clinton, Ohio.

That same day, the Jamestown Weekly Alert article, *Lake Erie's Sea Serpent Seen*, documented yet another close-up sighting, saying:

The other morning Adam Oper, a fisherman, and William Grubb, the light keeper at Pelee [Island], Toledo, [Ohio], both had a good view of the monster sea serpent that has frequently been seen in former seasons in Lake Erie. It raised its head near one of Oper's boats, and seemed to be about 30 feet long, with a disproportionately large head. A dorsal fin extended as far as the back could be seen, and when erected, was about 12 inches high. Horns much like a catfish was on either side of the head. Its underparts seemed white at first, but as the monster's rage at Oper increased, that portion turned a bright red. The back of the serpent seemed to be covered with scales. From the moment the head was raised it kept up a penetrating hiss, which could be heard for some distance. Oper sailed for the shore as fast as possible.

The August 6, 1897 The Owosso Times article, *Sea Serpent Appears Again,* documented yet another sighting, this time circling back to the description of saying the cryptid had a horse-like head, saying:

The sea serpent has appeared in Lake Erie. He was seen Tuesday at the lower end of Sugar [Island, Detroit]. The sea serpent is about [30] feet long and as big around as a barrel. The head, which is of a dark color, resembles in outline that of a horse. It was seen some distance off shore and was going in an easterly direction. The serpent was in view for a considerable time, but finally disappeared beneath the waves.

The shape of the head changed again in the July 17, 1931 The Indianapolis Times article, *30-foot Sea Serpent in Lake Erie,* which recorded that:

Erie navigators today were on the lookout for a 30-foor sea serpent reported sighted by at least ten persons.

H. E. Welsh, a fisherman, told of seeing the serpent while fishing from a small boat. He said he first thought the "monster" was a row of small kegs in the water, but discovered his mistake when it raised a huge head resembling that of an alligator.

Campers near the mouth of Portage [River] verified Welsh's story. They said they saw the serpent in the river not far from Port Clinton. Jacob Teasel, Sandusky fisherman, lent further credence to the reports when he told of seeing "something like a huge limb" in the Sandusky [River] before Fremont, [Ohio].

"The serpent must be at least [30] feet long," Teasel said. "We didn't take time to haul anchor, but cut the rope and rowed ashore as fast as we could."

It was spotted again and documented in the July 21, 1934 The Waterbury Democrat article, *Ohio Has a Sea Serpent Scare*, which said that:

A "sea serpent" 20 feet long and with a head as large as a dog's, was reported off of the popular Edgewater water bathing beach [in Cleveland, Ohio] on a Monday after a busy weekend's swimming and lolling.

Ben A. Schwartz saw the "serpent" and would verify his story. "I'm not trying to tell a fish story," said Schwartz. "We saw this thing swimming toward shore and thought at first it was a dog. Then it turned around and we got a good look at it. It was some kind of water snake."

Schwartz affirmed the monstrosity swam about near the beach for 15 minutes, then headed toward deeper water.

Parks director August Kurdziel said he would have the beach inspected by life guards. Cleveland Museum of Natural History officials said the snake might have been a rock python that had escaped from captivity somewhere, but point out that snakes of that size are not native to Lake Erie.

After interest in the Loch Ness Monster began and cryptozoology became captured by young Earth creationism, people began reporting a more plesiosaurus body, even though they became extinct in the Cretaceous period.

BIGFOOT

A lso referred to as Sasquatch, this popular cryptid has an expansive history, but seems to be a mixture of wild man legends across cultures.

Explored in Douglas Perry's The Oregonian January 25, 2018 article, *How a 1924 Bigfoot battle on Mt. St. Helens helped launch a legend*, this cryptid first captured America's imagination when, in 1924, gold prospectors Fred Beck, Gabe Lefever, John Peterson, Marion Smith and Smith's son Roy had been staying in a cabin situated in a narrow gorge on the eastern side of the mountain, near Spirit Lake, when "gorilla men" began trying to destroy the structure by throwing large stones.

They described them as walking on hind legs, being "covered with long, black hair", "ears are about four inches long and stick straight up", having "four toes, short and stubby", and weighing about 400 pounds. Beck shot and killed one, leading the assault to occur, one of the creatures even ripped a hole into the roof to get to the man. When the sun rose, the creatures left, and the men escaped and informed authorities at the closest town of the incident. Rangers J.H. Huffman and William Welch found no evidence of the cryptids and concluded the stones had been thrown by other prospectors to scare the men away.

According to Jorg Totsgi's The Oregonian July 15, 1924 article, *Big Hairy Indians Back of Ape Tale*, the indigenous persons in and around the area identified these creatures as members of the Seeahtik tribe, and goes on to write that:

> Oregon and Washington [indigenous persons] agree that the Seeahtik ... are [no] less than seven feet tall and some have been seen that were fully eight feet in height. They have hairy bodies like the bear. This is to protect them from the cold as they live entirely in the

mountains. They kill their game entirely by hypnotism. They have great supernatural powers. They also have the gift of ventriloquism, and have deceived many ordinary [indigenous persons] by throwing their voices.

[The Seeahtik] talk, beside the bear language of the [Klallam people], the bird language ... [They] can imitate any bird of the northwest, especially the blue jay. And that they have a very keen sense of smell ... The Puget Sound [indigenous persons] say they live in the heart of Vancouver Island, [British Columbia].

Totsgi went on to share the experience of Henry Napoleon who had been visiting relatives of the Cowichan people in Duncan, British Columbia, when he encountered one of the Seeahtik. He said the Seeahtik person spoke to him in his own language and he followed them on "an underground trail and after a few hours of travel" came to a large cave where the people lived throughout winter. The visitor also remarked that "the reason they were not seen very much was because they had a strange medicine that they rubbed over their bodies so that it made them invisible" and also utilized their "wha-ktee-aee-sing", or hypnotism, for the same purposes.

In Jorg Totsgi's follow-up July 17 article in the same paper, *Ape Hunt to Fail, Indians Predict*, he went on to say that Klallam people call them "Typanish" and that the Tsihalis people called them "Nung-nung", and that:

[The Seeahtik] generally make their appearance around Mt. Saint Helens the latter part of July and as a general rule do not remain there very long. Then they move north to the Olympic range, where they do their fall fishing in the upper parts of [Lake] Quinault and the Brinnon River.

Then about the first of November or with the first breath of winter they start their southward journey to Vancouver Island, where they remain during the entire winter.

Totsgi went on to share the experience of Allen Chenois who said that his uncle described them as:

"... They were tall, narrow-hipped and had crooked legs, and at the same time were deep-chested with heavy arms and enormous hands. They were covered with thick hair and had large breasts. Their heads were matted with uncut hair and black glittering eyes like the eyes of birds. Their jaws were massive .... They were so strong it is known they could pull a grown man's head right off."

He also wrote about their origin, saying:

Tradition of the Pacific coast [indigenous people] bears out the fact that [the Seeahtik] were animals at one time, and during the process of evolution when they were changing from the animal to man, [they] did not absorb the [tamahnous] or soul power, and thus they became an anomaly in the process of evolution.

J. W. Burns, a First Nation teacher living in the Sts'ailes Nation of British Columbia published his investigation into the lore about wild man sightings in his April 1, 1929 MacLean's Magazine entry, *Introducing B.C.'s Hairy Giants*, and was the first to use the word "sasquatch".

He wrote that Peter Williams, who lived on the Chehalis Reserve, encountered what he first thought was "a huge bear crouched on a bolder" that "except that he was covered with hair and twice the bulk of the average men, there was nothing to distinguish him from the rest of us". Williams went on to say that the nude wild man "grunted like an animal" when attempting to cause damage to his home later. The next morning, Williams recalled that he had "found his tracks in the mud around the house, the biggest of either man or beast ... [which] measured [22"] in length, but narrow".

He continued with the account of Charley Victor on the Skwah Reserve, who had told him that they were called Sasquatch, weren't First Nation, and that he had been "bathing in a small lake near Yale" when he encountered "a nude hairy man" that "walked into the forest". Victor went on to say that on one occasion, he had been hunting "in the mountains near Hatzie" when thinking he was shooting a bear, discovered he had shot a nude white teenage boy, but that "his hair was black and wooly" who called out. He went on to describe the boy's companion, saying:

> "The hairy creature, for that was what it was, walked toward me without the slightest fear. The wild person was a woman. Her face was almost ... black and her long straight hair fell to her waist. In height she would have been about six feet, but her chest and shoulders were well above the average in breadth.

> She cast a glance at the boy. Her face took on a demonical expression when she saw he was bleeding. She turned upon me savagely, and in the Douglas tongue said, 'You have shot my friend.'

> I explained in the same langue – for I'm part Douglas myself – that I had mistaken the boy for a bear and that I was sorry. She did not reply, but began a sort of wild frisk or dance around the boy, chanting in a loud voice for a

minute or two, and, as if in answer to her, from the distant woods came the same sort of chanting troll. In her hand she carried something like a snake, about six feet in length, but thinking over the matter since, I believe it was the intestine of some animal. But whatever it was, she constantly struck the ground with it. She picked up the boy with one hairy hand, with as much ease as if he had been a wax doll."

He went on to explain that she had pointed the intestine at her, told her that he would never shoot a bear, again, and years later, he suffered a stroke that prevented him from hunting anymore. She had also said the word "Yahoo" many times during the encounter.

Burns called the creatures "sasq'ets", which others have translated from the Halq'emeylem language to mean "hairy man" or "tree man", however, Brent Douglas Galloway's 2009 book, *Dictionary of Upriver Halkomelem*, explains that it means "to crack on the back".

According to Eric Bailey's Los Angeles Times April 19, 2003 article, *Bigfoot's Big Feat*, the term "big foot" was used by logging company employees working with prankster Jerry Crew, who, unknown to them, had been leaving sasquatch tracks in the mud north of Willow Creek in Six Rivers National Forest, California in 1958. He had done so by attaching a large "set of carved alder-wood feet to stomp the footprints". Plaster casts were taken of the footprints, and public interest in the cryptid was renewed.

Boojum

The boojum of western North Carolina is said to inhabit caves on the Eaglenest Mountain in Haywood County. According to the July - December 2011 edition of *The Journal of Spelean History*, originally, the creature was a wild man who hid his precious jewels at the bottom of moonshine jugs in stories told by S. C. Satterthwaitee who built the 40-room Eagle's Nest Hotel on the mountain in 1899. Its name was taken from Lewis Carroll's 1876 nonsensical poem, *The Hunting of the Snark*, where it's a highly dangerous creature.

The creature's story soon spread to the Great Balsam Mountains and appeared in Buncombe, Henderson, Transylvania, Haywood, and Jackson counties. Revealed in Visit NC Smokies blog entry, *The Legend of the Balsam Mountains Boojum*, there is a folktale where a wild man and a local girl named Annie fell in love and lived in a cave.

On November 15, 1987, the *Asheville Citizen-Times* documented his change into "somewhat akin to the Abominable Snow Man of the Himalayas", aligning with the more popular image of bigfoot.

Potter Nondescript

According to *The Potter Enterprise's* April 28, 1897 edition, William Butler was reported to have the best description of the strange creature spotted that year in Potter County, Pennsylvania, by documenting:

> *Though under the circumstances his eyes might have magnified a little, he thinks the animal was fully six feet high when standing on its hind legs. It was quite hairy about the head and had tusks from six to seven inches long, which the animal seemed proud to show, and another such mouth was never seen ... Bill looked at the Potter County nondescript fully a minute or more.*

This was a week after an unnamed fisherman had been chased by a hairy creature that was beating its chest. Butler, too, said that when he saw the creature, it was eating a groundhog, and chased him away by beating its chest.

Slothfoot

The well-known story of a wild man in Okefenokee Swamp in Ware County, Georgia has evolved from being reimagined as a sasquatch to being seized by those with young Earth creationist ideology to transform the original story into a sighting of a giant called a nephilim or giant ground sloth that died out 11,000 years ago.

The tale was documented in the January 1829 edition of the *Statesman* but was picked up by other newspapers in surrounding states, documenting:

Not long ago, two men and a boy, in the vicinity of this swamp, like our friend Paul Pry, "had a curiosity to know, you know," what could be seen by two or three weeks pilgrimage into the accessible regions of this dismal empire. The season being unusually dry, they pushed their exploration far into the interior, and at the end of little more than two weeks, found their progress suddenly arrested at the appearance of the print of a foot step, so unearthly in its dimensions, so ominous of power, and terrible in form, that they were at once reminded of the legend we have mentioned above, and began seriously to apprehend its solemn reality. The length of the foot was eighteen, and the breadth nine inches. The monster, from every appearance, must have moved forward in an easy or hesitating gait; his stride, from heel to toe, being but a trifle over six feet. Our adventurers had seen enough and began to think of securing a retreat, without waiting to salute his majesty, not doubting but the other part of the story might also prove true - of his fierceness and cruelty. They happily [affected] their escape, returned home and related the history of their adventures, and what they had seen of the "man mountain." A company of Florida hunters, half horse and half alligator - nine in number, determined, a few months since, to make this gentleman a visit - to ascertain if he had a family, and his manner of living. Following, for some days, the direction of their guide, they came at length upon the track first discovered; some vestiges of which were still remaining; pursuing these traces several days longer they came to a half on a little eminence, and determined to pitch their camp and refresh themselves for the day. The report of their rifles, as one or two of them were simultaneously discharged at an advancing and ferocious wild beast, made the still solitudes of these dismal lakes [reverberate] with deafening roar. Echo beyond echo, took up and prolonged the sound, which seemed to die away and revive in successive peals for several minutes. The report had reached and startled from his lair, the genius of the swamp, and the next minute he was full in their view, advancing upon them with a terrible look and a ferocious mien. Our little band, instinctively gathered close in a body, and presented their rifles. The huge being, nothing daunted, bounded upon his victims, and in the same instant received the contents of seven rifles. But he did not fall alone; nor until he had glutted his wrath with the death of five of them, which he effected by [ringing] off the head from the body. Writhing and exhausted at length he fell, with his hapless prey beneath his grasp. The surviving four had opportunity to examine the dreadful being as he lay extended on the earth, some time, wallowing and roaring.

His length was thirteen feet, and his breadth and volume of just proportions. Fearing, lest the report of their rifles, and the stentorian yells of the expiring giant, should bring suddenly upon them the avengers of his blood, they betook themselves to flight, having first secured the rifles of their headless comrades, and returned home with this account of their adventures.

The story of the report, as related above, is matter of fact, and the truth of it is accredited, we are told, by persons living on the borders of this swamp, and in the neighborhood of the surviving adventurers.

Many books, including Frank Hendersen's 2023's *Bigfoot in Georgia*, as well as many websites omit large parts of the initial story to correlate the wild man to a bigfoot.

Cryptid Wiki's entry, *Slothfoot*, includes the evolution of the wild man into a giant ground sloth, citing a witness named Henry who wrote:

I caught sight of a large animal moving through the cypress trees of the swampy area that borders one of the fields I work. I live in Ware County, Georgia. I was working the field at the time and noticed the movement. It was late afternoon and still light out. The animal was huge, hairy and walked on all fours but I did see it rear up once. It reminded me of a black bear but much larger and lighter in color. I was about 200 [yards] away from it but I still had a good look. I know for a fact that this was not a bear. I've seen black bears in the Okefenokee and this didn't look like one of those at all. I later saw a picture of an animal, a mapinguari, that is supposed to be a legend. I swear that is what I saw. Have you heard of this animal? I haven't seen it since but there have been a lot of cypress trees tore up lately and I'm wondering if it has been causing it. Some people have said for many years that there's a swamp beast in Ware County but I never paid it no mind until now.

The Mapinguari is a hairy humanoid in Brazilian folklore which was been reimagined as a giant ground sloth because it was said to have a gaping mouth in its abdomen, which those outside of the culture imagined must have been a marsupium, or the pouch where newborns live and nurse.

White Bigfoot of Belmont, New York

According to Mason Winfield's Buffalo Rising October 31, 2015 article, *The Thirteen Creepies of the Western Door*, this albino bigfoot, also called the Black Creek Whodat of Allegany County, began to be spotted in 1973 near "near Lost Nation and Black Creek" communities.

Wild Man of Ohio

The Midland Journal's March 11, 1887 article, *The Wild Man of Ohio*, documents a hair wild man, saying:

A party of hunters, who have just returned from a hunt in the hills of Holmes County, Ohio, say they encountered a curious creature on their trip. According to their description, a wild man, or some strange being, is at large in Holmes County. The part who report seeing the strange creature claim that he or it looked like a man, but acted like a wild beast. The creature was encountered near a brushy thicket and willow copse near that is known as Big Spring, where General Buell rested on his march through Ohio, at a point a short distance south of the Wayne County line in Holmes County. The hunters were beating the brush for pheasants when the attention of one of the party was attracted to an object that suddenly darted across an opening in the brush. Later on the object was again seen along the edge of the brush. By this time the hunters had reached open ground, and were surprised to see what they describe as a man, entirely nude, but covered with what appeared to them to be matter hair. When seen he was some distance away, but on discovering the hunters he started toward them on a run, and gave forth queer guttural sounds. On seeing the strange being moving toward them they part of hunters, which included four persons, all armed with shot guns, broke and ran. The strange creature pursued them for a short distance until the party had reached a public highway, when he turned back and was seen to enter Killbuck Creek, which he swam, and then disappeared in the brush again. On approaching the water he dropped on all fours and plunged in like a dog, swimming in a manner similar to a canine. The hunters did not have the nerve to return, but got away from the place as soon as possible.

This is one of the few accounts of a sasquatch-like creature swimming.

Wild Man of Western North Carolina

Luke Manget's The Southern Highlander's entry, *Wild Man of the Woods*, does an excellent job of exploring the folklore surrounding the precursor to both sasquatch and feral people of the Smokey Mountains, and explains why so many vanishing caves were said to contain the bones of "giants".

Lore explained that they were "giant" feral people resembling the classic depiction of a caveman, almost seeming like a mix between animal and man, and were feral and dangerous to anyone who encountered them.

The first page of *The Wilmington Morning Star's* December 15, 1877, for instance, ran an article claiming:

A wild man of the mountains has been seen in Watauga County, [North Carolina]. He made tracks, and has not since been seen. The Landmark says: Our correspondent describes the man as being about six feet five inches tall, with broad shoulders and long [ape-like] arms; smooth face and funnel-shaped head. His body is covered with dark brown hair, near two inches long. His head and a greater portion of his forehead is covered with long, luxuriant, dark red tresses. Our correspondent affirms that this is the first time this wild man has ever been seen or heard of in the neighborhood.

However, on December 16, *The Charlotte Observer* retracted this story:

The Piedmont Press denies the Statesville Landmark's story about the wild man of Watauga County. It says that people living in the neighborhood where the alleged wild man is said to have been seen, never saw or heard of him except though the newspapers.

Manget's entry says that that same year, gold miners in Caldwell County, North Carolina encountered a wild man with the same appearance. When he saw the miners, the wild man pounded his chest and ran into the woods at the speed of a deer. The men tracked him into a cave deep in the woods, where they found many animal bones indicating that the wild man had lived inside for a long time.

Between the publication of the June 1, 1890 Chattanooga Daily Times article, *A Wild Man*, and the 1896 journal, *Forest and Stream*, Mason Evans, an elderly man who had lived alone in the mountains of Tennessee for possibly 40 years, became transformed into a monster for readers. The journal claimed that he had talon-like fingernails and toenails, "tusks instead of teeth", and long hair.

Woodbooger of Virginia and Tennessee

According to Gregg MacDonald's October 2022 Cooperative Living entry, *The Legend of the Woodbooger*, this is the title given to bigfoot in southwest Virginia and northeast Tennessee. Further into Tennessee, it is also called the Tennessee Wildman.

Yayho of West Virginia

First appearing in *The Times Leader's* October 26, 1973 edition, and then in Jim F. Comstock's 1974 book, *West Virginia Songbag*, this is the name given to bigfoot in West Virginia.

BLUE DEVIL DOG OF GRASSY CREEK

D etailed in Clio's entry, *'Blue Devil' Scare of 1939-1940*, that winter, a "blue-skinned" or "blue faced" canine the size of a "pony" was blamed for killing livestock in Webster and Randolph counties. In December, John Clevenger's dog was killed and one of Ernest Cogar's cows and a sheep were killed. They and Mrs. V. S. Cunlip had heard a "wild, inhuman scream" that reminded them of a mountain lion that they attributed to the devil dog. It was shot and killed by Elmer Corley and was described as like a coyote, but not.

BUTLER GARGOYLE

A lso called the Chicora Mothman, it first appeared in Joedy Cook's 2014, *Mothman Casebook*, and later in Tyler Houck's 2018 book, *Cryptid U.S.*, it's described as a seven to eight feet tall, gray-skinned humanoid wearing a "bicycle helmet", and with bat-like wings or a cape. The humanoid was allegedly sighted between June 1993 and March 2011 in Allentown and Chicora, Pennsylvania.

CARMEL AREA CREATURE

According to Ron McGlone's December 19, 2014 Highland County Press article, *Strange creature reported in Carmel area*, an unnamed elderly husband and wife spotted a headless and armless, seven-foot-tall "slim gray creature with muscular legs that walked like its knees were backwards" on the road late one night.

CAYUGA LAKE MONSTER

L ocated in Cayuga, Seneca, and Tompkins counties, New York "Old Greeny" is described as a 15 to 35-feet-long serpentine scaly creature, and was first mentioned in the January 5, 1897 edition of *The Ithaca Journal*, where it was revealed that the cryptid was first spotted in 1828. The article goes on to say:

The members of The Journal staff have been living in daily anticipation of the monster's appearance, and have actually shunned assignments which would take them near the water's edge for fear of being compelled to shudder, and tremble at the sight of him ... [Old Greeny] waits until the cold north winds blow their chilly selves across the placid lake and ruffle its composure, until one would think that the lake itself is agitated by reason of its fearful guest. By selecting those times for his visit, the old boy knows that human courage cannot well brave the fury of a gale and the sight of him also, so he is safe.

The same article related an eyewitness who said:

"I was taking a pleasure drive this morning along the east shore of the lake with a friend, when I chanced to look out on the lake, and there about [200]-feet from the shore, I saw what at first glance filled me with fear, but at the same time riveted my gaze. I immediately guessed that it was the famed sea serpent. I quickly alighted from the carriage and with my companion walked to the shore. We were at McKinney's at the time. The head of the animal was large and its body long and it disported in seeming glee among the white caps. It was certainly the sea serpent. I never saw an animal of its description before and it tallied with accounts I have read of the serpent."

In the June 1, 1929 edition of the same newspaper, an article opening with "Cayuga Lake has been invaded by two mysterious 'sea serpents'" informed readers that two of the 12 – 15-foot long creatures had been spotted on the eastern shore.

The August 17, 2007 edition of the newspaper explores another sighting when Jack Marshall recalled that in 1979, he was boating with friends when he spotted "a huge serpentine beast floating on the surface of the lake". The group went on to describe it as between 30 and 35 feet long, and it submerged before their boat could get too close.

There have been no more sightings, but Old Greeny appears as an entry in many books on the supernatural.

COONCAT

Appearing in C. P. Marshall's 2024 book, *The Cryptozoology of Cats*, after accounts appeared online, it's described as a mixture of raccoon and cat and was reported sighted by teenagers in northwestern Georgia between 2013 and 2014.

COOSA RIVER
MONSTER

In his May 21, 2017 Rome News-Tribune article, *Monsters of the Coosa River*, Mike Ragland details the first encounters with one of these creatures, writing that:

> In 1816, a hunting party from St. Clair County, Alabama, was just below Ten Mile Island on the Coosa River. They stumbled upon a dead animal that was half in and half out of the water. One of the hunters later wrote a letter to his sister in Charleston about the beast. It would be over 50 years before the letter surfaced.

> It said when they cut the critter open, they found [an indigenous man], his canoe, a bow and arrows, a deer and a rifle. The writer said they figured the rifle was what made it sick and killed it. His description has stood through the years. He described it as a type of sea serpent, with scales, a long tail about 25 feet in length, and big around the middle.

He goes on to write that J. M. Elliott, a steamboat captain, had seen the creature several times.

In the June 6, 1877 edition of *The Gadsen Times* detailed various sightings of the cryptid, saying:

> As [Marcus L. Foster] approached near enough to see it distinctly, to his horror it proved to be a living monster or serpent, with head and neck erect, extending out of the water some three or four feet, its head resembling a horse's head, large glaring eyes and mouth distended showing a tongue of fiery red.

The monster or serpent showed no signs of fear, but glared directly at Foster as it passed, and unprepared as he was, he thought discretion the better part of valor and beat a hasty retreat to the opposite bank, from which he watched it moving along like a man in a boat, showing now and then portions of its back, until it reached a point opposite Thorton's log yard, where it gave a plunge and disappeared from sight.

Foster was an entirely trustworthy and reliable gentleman, well known in his community, and his statements could be relied upon. There was little doubt in his mind that he saw this monster. Because of the improbability, he was very reluctant to report the sighting.

The story never would have been reported if not for another sighting reported by a prominent individual.

[Captain] James M. Elliott, with another individual, was making an excursion in their pleasure boat about the same time, and saw a similar object below Rome moving along at a leisurely gait through the water, which they described as some 40 feet in length, and with a body as large as a hogshead.

A woman who lived on the Coosa for many years told Foster she had seen a similar creature some 15 years earlier.

Judge Lemuel J. Standifer, and old and highly respected citizen of this county, corroborated the statement of the woman. He had occasion to cross the river near Rome, and was paddling along in a canoe when he heard a noise like distant thunder that seemed to be just behind him. He turned his head and, in a deep hole that he had passed some 30 or 40 yards before, he saw a monster with a serpent head and enormous body erect some 14 or 15 feet above the water gradually sink until it disappeared.

The newspaper concluded that all the sightings were masses of decomposing leaves that had fallen into the river.

DEVIL MONKEY
OF VIRGINIA

D ocumented in his 2012 book, *Monsters of Virginia*, L. B. Taylor, Jr. tells the story of an unnamed woman traveling through Roanoke, Virginia from Ohio to the Outer Banks of North Carolina when she was stopped when a six-foot-tall, monkey-wolf hybrid with "short sleek black fur", pointed ears, and a long thin tail on a lonely two-lane road.

DEVIL'S CONSTRICTORS

T he term "Devil's Constrictor" seems to first have been mentioned in a probable satirical Uncoveror entry, *Another Danger at Red River Gorge*, where it is described as a dangerous breed of anaconda-sized winged snake:

> *This beast has been known to creep up on unsuspecting victims and jump on them, constricting them to their demise. Reports of this creature measuring up to twenty feet in length, and having the ability to glide from the trees up to one hundred feet away have made their way into the local culture, however, no empirical evidence has been found to support these claims.*

The tale of flying snakes in Kentucky began with The Evening Bulletin May 23, 1899 article, *A Vanceburg Snake Story*, which reveals:

> *John Greenert, a prominent farmer of the Tygart Creek neighborhood [of Vanceburg], whose veracity has never been doubted, tells of a wonderful species of winged snake seen by him and a farm-hand on his place. He described the snake, which they first discovered lying on the ground, as about three feet long and ten inches in circumference at the center. It had four pairs of legs, two near the head and two just back of the wings, which grew just forward of the middle body. The wings consisted of a membranous substance which, when the snake was in a dormant condition, remained folded up under the body and were not noticed by them until on their approach. With a spring it raised from the ground and sailed through the air at a terrific speed. The snake is as black as charcoal and has a very repulsive appearance, especially when flying through*

the air. As Mr. Greenert lives in the neighborhood of the Carter Caves it is supposed that his snakeship's hiding place is in the cakes.

In the first part of his two-part series about winged snakes titled *Myth of menace?*, and published in The Advocate-Messenger on March 15, 2009, Nick Sucik documents an earlier sighting of one of these reptiles. He wrote that in 1895, Roger Watson was hunting the Parksville community in western Boyle County when he saw a group of the reptiles "flying above the tops of bushes". He shot one that "measured at 18 inches in length [and] was black and had wings like a bat". Those who saw the specimen agreed it was a snake, and there was no mention of legs like in Greenert's account. Sucik went on to write that:

Of its six bordering states, at least four had newspaper accounts reporting their own flying snakes. In fact, between 1823 and 1917, there were at least 27 instances of newspapers featuring flying snake sightings.

In his conclusion article in the same newspaper on March 22, 2009 in the article, *Winged snakes seen throughout the U.S.*, he documented historical sightings and concluded that because of indigenous mythology about winged or feathered serpents, the species must have some basis in reality.

DOGMAN

R evealed in Emily Bingham's September 4, 2020 MyNorth entry, *Q&A*, the creature was invented in 1987 by Steve Cook, a disc jockey at WTCM-FM in Traverse City, Michigan as an April Fool's Day joke. All parts of the legend, including its 1887 Wexford County, Michigan, appearance, were part of his satirical song, "The Legend", played that night.

Dana Rehn's blog entry, *What is the meaning behind the dog-man conjoined twins in the Nuremberg Chronicle?*, explains that, in the past, dogman represented someone who had secretly converted from Christianity to the Islamic faith, or represented "barbarous" pagans opposed to Christianity.

The story of "The Beast of the Land between the Lakes" in Kentucky, presented as a dogman, seems to have been the invention of Jan Thompson when she submitted her *Jan's Tales* to San Perry's website in 2002. She wrote that she was working at a gas station in the 1980s and one night two police officers told her that four victims had been torn apart by the beast in the national park. The tale was expanded on by Lyle Russell. In Erin McCullough's October 23, 2023 WKRN article, *Haunted Legends*, Russell claimed to have met a man named Roger, an alleged survivor of the massacre.

The original radio broadcast may have led to the legend of the Beast of Bray Road, a werewolf that inspired Linda Godfrey to write *The Beast of Bray Road* in 2015. In January 1992 of that year, reports of a strange wolf that some said walked on its hind legs began circulating. Longtime residents of the area didn't believe the tales.

EASTERN COUGARS

According to Cassandra Yorgey's February 17, 2023 Exemplore expose, *Experts deny population of cougars in Appalachian Mountains*, officially, mountain lions vanished from the mountain range sometime in the 1940s, and are considered "extinct" in the Southern Appalachian Mountains. However, not everyone believed that. In fact, "big cat" sightings of cougars, black mountain lions, and even a cat-like beast known as the "Appalachian Chupacabra" have continued since they were allegedly hunted out of existence.

Black catamounts have appeared in folklore, even though there's little evidence for their existence. A typical story for why they're allegedly in the mountains usually involves a circus train car accident, at an unknown location, that released them into the area sometime in the remote past.

According to the Wildlife Resources Agency's article, *Cougars in Tennessee*, "no black color phase (termed melanistic) of a cougar has ever been documented". The website goes on to say that black jaguars have been documented in South America and Mexico.

However, these aren't regular big cats with black fur. The proposed species in the mountains are smaller than a mountain lion, which can weigh up to 175 pounds, or a jaguar, which can weigh up to 300 pounds.

This type of big cat is typically described as "as big as a spaniel", similar to the propertied size of fabled British big cats such as the Beast of Buchan in Aberdeenshire, Scotland, and the Beast of Bodmin Moor and the Beast of Exmoor, in the United Kingdom.

According to an October 28, 1963 Covington Virginian article, *"Mystery Beast" Appears Again At Clifton Forge*, multiple residents, including a member of law enforcement, saw a "mysterious beast" that is described as one of these big black cougars, after it was documented "biting chunks out of" Carl Drew's livestock.

The article continues by saying that when Deputy Sheriff Robert Williams responded to a call about the feline attacking the Webb family's dog, he had a close encounter with the beast. He said that, on the way to the residence, it jumped over his car. He stopped and saw that it was crouched in the grass off the side of the road. He reported that when he fired at it, it jumped a few feet off of the ground and ran off.

Both Mr. Webb and Deputy Williams described the creature as having a body about four-feet-long, not including a three-foot tail, weighing somewhere between 40 and 60 pounds, and dark to black hair. A manhunt didn't locate the beast, and the animal attacks soon faded into obscurity.

This supposed smaller species has been called "the Appalachian Chupacabra" more recently, having behavior similar to the beast of Puerto Rican folklore while preying on livestock.

The most publicized mountain lion attack was the "vampire beast of Bladenboro", North Carolina.

Revealed in John Gause's January 5, 1954 The Robesonian article, *Armed Hunting Party To Seek Bladenboro's 'Vampire Beast'*, after more deaths of family dogs were reported, local police chief Roy Forbes began working with several armed citizens with bloodhounds to hunt down the mysterious beast. The creature was first sighted by a man named Lloyd Clemons, who described it as "around three-feet-long, and low to the ground, probably 18 – 24-inches height", and sounded like a cat. The article speculates that it could be a mountain lion that weighed anywhere between 80 and 100 pounds, as two or three witnesses had described it as being cat-like.

The next notable newspaper entry about this creature was Clyde Osborne's January 7 The Charlotte Observer article, *Bladen Beast Hunt Hampered*. The beast attempted to attack the wife of

C. E. Kinlaw until he scared it away. She had gone out around 8:00 PM to investigate the sounds of a dog in distress. The couple couldn't determine if the creature was a large dog or a large cat.

While the News and Record's December 17, 1954 article, *Big Mongrel Dog Killed, Ending Scare Reports*, explains that the deaths of so many dogs were the result of a "huge gray dog an 80-pound mongrel" that was 80-pounds and leading a pack of wild dogs and killed on the farm of Marvin McLamb, the News and Observer April 27, 1958 article, *Another Beast On the Prowl?*, says that a similar beast was stalking Atlanta, Georgia and that it, like the Bladenboro beast, "was generally concluded to be a panther, although a Mexican ocelot and a bobcat were tracked down and killed later".

FLATWOODS
MONSTER

Outlined in Frank Feschino, Jr.'s 2013 book, *The Braxton County Monster*, this proposed extraterrestrial appeared on September 12, 1952, after a "bright light" was spotted falling from the sky onto G. Bailey Fisher's farmland. Brothers Edward and Fred May, their friend Tommy Hyer, two other children Neil Nunley and Ronnie Shaver, Kathleen May, and West Virginia National Guardsman Eugene Lemon went to investigate the assumed meteorite and spotted a creature that they described as ten-feet-tall with a bloody red round face with glowing greenish-orange, a spade-like cape, "small, claw-like hands", and a metal skirt that allowed it to glide. The group said that a pungent smell had caused them to become ill, and reported the encounter to local authorities.

FLYING RAYS

R evealed in Linda S. Godfrey's 2014 book, *American Monsters*, flying manta rays and stingrays first appeared on Lon Strickler's *Phantoms & Monsters* blog, contributed by sometimes anonymous persons. They were described as large as cars, appearing as they do in the ocean or as semi-transparent, and moving through the air with "a swimming motion". One of the most celebrated sightings was in 2004, near the Ohio River near Point Pleasant, West Virginia, linking it to "high strangeness" associated with the Mothman. These posts were also repeated in T. S. Mart's 2021 book, *A Guide to Sky Monsters*.

GIANT RATTLESNAKE
OF HARLAN

In August 1857, many newspapers picked up the story, originally appearing in the *Abingdon Democrat*, about a monstrous rattlesnake allegedly killed in Harlan County, Kentucky, saying:

About three weeks ago, five men when to gather whortleberries in the mountainous parts of Harlan [County], Kentucky, and in their travels came to a small branch, at the foot of a steep ridge, where they discovered a smooth beaten path, or rather slide, that led from the branch to the ridge. Curiosity tempted them to know its meaning, and they followed the trail to the top of the ridge, where, to their astonishment, they found about an acre of grand perfectly smooth and destitute of vegetation, near the center of which they discovered a small sink or cave, large enough to admit a barrel. They concluded to drop in a few stones, and presently their ears were saluted with a loud rumbling sound, accompanied with a rattling noise, and an enormous serpent made his appearance, blowing and spreading his head, and his forked tongue protruded. The men were struck with wonder and [afraid], and suddenly the atmosphere was filled with a smell so nauseating that three out of five were taken very sick; the other two, discovering the condition of their companions, dragged them away from that abode of death.

About ten feet of the snake had to their judgement made its appearance, when they hurried home and related what they had seen to their neighbors.

The next day were mounted some ten of the hardy mountaineers, armed with rifles, determined to destroy the monster. On approaching within [100] yards of the dwelling of his snakeship, their horses suddenly became restive, and neither kindness nor force could make them go any nearer. The men dismounted, and hitching their horses, proceeded on foot, with rifles cocked, to the mouth of the cave. They hurled in three or four large stones, and fell back some [15] steps, when the same noise was heard as before, and out came the dreaded reptile, ready as his looks indicated to crush the intruders. About the same length of the snake had appeared from the hole, when eight or ten bullets went through his head, and, as the monster died, he kept crawling out, until [20] feet of that huge boa lay motionless on the ground. It was a rattlesnake, with 28 rattles – the first was four inches in diameter, the rest decreasing in size to the last. With difficulty then men dragged him home, and his skin can now be seen by the curious, in Harlan [County].

David Mikkelson's July 8, 2010 Snopes entry, *15-Foot Eastern Diamondback Rattlesnake*, explains that the eastern diamondback rattler can grow up to about eight feet.

GOOSEFOOT

A lso called the Cumberland Dragon, this Georgia and Tennessee cryptid was seemingly spotted only once, and documented in the *Caledonian Mercury* on December 4, 1794, which read:

On February last, a detachment of mounted infantry, commanded by Captain John Beard, penetrated fifteen miles into the Cumberland Mountain.

On Cover Creek, Ensign McDonald and another man, in advance of the party as spies, discovered a creature about three steps from them; it had only two legs, and stood almost upright, covered with scales of a black, brown, and a light yellow [color] in spots like rings, a white tuft or crown on the top of its head, about four feet high, a head as big as a two pound stone, and large eyes of a fiery red.

It stood about three minutes in a daring posture (orders being given not to fire a gun except at the [indigenous persons].) Mr. McDonald advanced, and struck at it with his sword, when it jumped at least eight feet, and lit on the same spot of ground, sending forth a red kind of matter out of its mouth, resembling blood, and then retreated into a laurel thicket, turning round often as if it intended to fight.

The tracks of it resembled that of a goose, but larger.

The [indigenous people] report that a creature inhabits that part of the mountain of the above description, which, by its breath, will kill a man, if he does not instantly immerse himself in water.

Various authors have transformed this description to meet a more modern interpretation of what a dragon appears as in pop culture.

GRAFTON MONSTER

A ccording to David Sibray's June 13, 2018 West Virginia Explorer's article, *June 16 marks anniversary of Grafton Monster sightings*, in June 1964, about 20 different persons reported seeing the "Beast of Grafton" in Taylor County. Seemingly, they all described a humanoid that was about nine feet tall and four feet wide, had white "seal skin", and had no head but eyes "in the middle of its chest".

HERRINGTON LAKE MONSTER

L ocated in Boyle, Mercer and Garrard counties, Kentucky, the lake is said to be the home of "Herry" and "eel-pig" that is said to have a 20-foot-long eel-like body, have skin similar to a speckled fish, and swim faster than a boat. While internet sources claim the sightings have occurred since the lake was formed in 1925, the "monsters" referred to in newspapers were larger than expected fish.

Joe Ward's The Courier-Journal August 7, 1972 article, *'Monster' reported swimming in Herrington Lake*, is the first sighting of this creature, and details Lawrence S. Thomson's sighting "in the quiet stretch of water between Chenault Bridge and Wells Landing". The article goes on to explain that he had a house on the lake and that, "All he's ever seen is a snout – not unlike that of a pig, moving along just above the water at about the speed of a boat with a trolling motor – and a curly tail, similar to that of the same animal, coming along about 15 feet behind".

Kaye Coyte interviewed Thomson two years later, and in The Kentucky Kernel's February 13, 1974 article, *Creature of catfish?*, he said that "the thing could have been an alligator" and, "Then again it could be a giant catfish – they have been known to grow up to 12 feet".

Another sighting was documented in Sarah E. Upshaw's February 16, 1990 The Advocate-Messenger article, *Herrington Lake 'monster' causes quite a ripple, leaves lake residents speculating*, where Sherri Hurst, visiting her friend who lived on the shores of the lake "suddenly noticed a long, glittering dark shadow floating in the middle of the lake". Upshaw went on to write that:

The two women watched the shape swimming in a circle for at least 15 minutes. After submerging and rising several times, it finally went over to the shade of the opposite bank … "It was too big to be a gar," Hurt's friend said. She did suggest it could have been an overgrown catfish.

Since this sighting, Herry hasn't been seen but was covered in George Dudding's 2015 book, *Kentucky's Herrington Lake Monster.*

KENTUCKY GOBLINS

ocumented in Isabel Davis' 2018 book, *Close Encounters at Kelly and Others Of 1955*, on the evening of August 21, 1955, in Christian County, Kentucky, Elmer Sutton and Billy Ray Taylor claimed to have shot at what the media termed "little green men" trying to invade the cabin they were living in with others for nearly four hours before going to the local police department to report the incident.

Earlier in the evening, Taylor had seen a saucer-shaped craft land near the property. Soon, some of the seven children inside began seeing small goblin-like extraterrestrials wearing metallic "spacesuits" that were glowing peering into bedroom windows. All five adults barricaded themselves inside after seeing the group of aliens. Sutton and Taylor shot the figures repeatedly, but the bullets seemed to only stun them, and they would float down to the ground like falling leaves.

KENTUCKY LIZARDMAN

Mentioned in passing in Jeffrey his 2008 book, *Weird Kentucky*, Scott Holland wrote about this "lizard man" that:

In 1966, there was a sighting of a bipedal lizard-man in Stephensport, near where Sinking Creek meets the Ohio River. Described as 'very amphibious looking' and covered in brownish green scales, the creature appeared outside a home late at night and ran off into the darkness on its hind legs when confronted.

More details about this sighting appear in the Kentucky Bigfoot Research Organization's entry, *The Kentucky Lizardman*, where the experiencer was a man named Joseph who wrote:

When I was around [nine] years old living in Breckenridge County I had the most hairy raising experience of my life! One night while fast asleep in my bed I woke to a loud commotion outside my bedroom window, as if something hit the side of my house. I sprang to the window and looked out but saw nothing. So I ran to the living room and pulled back the curtains to the window of the front door and came face to face with the most strangest creature! I can only best describe it as a "lizard-man," although the only "human" thing about it was the fact that it stood on two legs and was about 5'6" to 6' tall! As you could image we really startled each other! It quickly turned and ran for the creek next to my house and I jumped back from the window! I then ran to an adjacent window to catch a glimpse of it as it ran away on two legs towards the creek which was about 75 yards from my house. I lost sight of it as it disappeared into the darkness.

The creature wasn't reported by other persons.

LAKE NORMAN
MONSTER

Nicknamed "Normie", this lake monster resides in Lake Norman in Iredell County, Catawba County, Mecklenburg County and Lincoln counties, North Carolina, and is described as "North Carolina's Loch Ness Monster" with a long serpentine-like body with scaly fins or flippers, a giant catfish, or an overgrown alligator.

The first mention of the creature was in a *Statesville Record and Landmark* September 29, 1995 article, where the local Lake Norman Balloon Company created a "Normy" balloon for a local parade. Previous accounts of "monsters" in the lake, created in 1964, were larger than expected fish.

MOTHMAN

First introduced in Gray Barker's 1970 book, *The Silver Bridge*, and expanded upon in John A. Keel's 1975 book, *The Mothman Prophecies*, the cryptid was described as seven-foot-tall dark, headless, "slender, muscular" bird-man with dark wings, and with glowing red eyes on its chest that seemed closely connected to a former World War II munitions plant just outside of Point Pleasant, West Virginia where it was originally spotted by two young couples on November 1966. It terrorized dozens of people, some reporting it as making a screeching sound, living in and around the town until the collapse of the Silver Bridge in December 1967, when it seemingly vanished. The sudden disappearance caused some to believe that it was an antemortem apparition foretelling the destruction of the bridge and the deaths of 46 persons.

MUD MERMAIDS
OF OHIO RIVER

D espite their name, these reptilian human were first documented in the News and Citizen's October 18, 1894 article, *Mud Mermaids*, where they were described quite differently from the modern image of mermaids:

On the sand bar in the Ohio [River] near Vevay, [Indiana], reside two nondescript creatures horrible in appearance and habit. They are amphibious in nature and resemble in appearance huge lizards with human features. When partly submerged in the yellow waters of the Ohio, they are strangely like human beings. Of what species of animal they are no one knows, for it is impossible to get near enough to them to judge correctly. The sand bar in question at low tide is covered with huge logs and stumps of trees, known in the river vernacular as snags. They have been deposited by the government snag boats engaged in keeping the channel clear. When the water is high enough to cover these snags, the creatures make their home among them. When the water receded, they disappear into some unknown lair and wait for a rise.

From identification they appear to be carnivorous. Among the snags are to be found wagon loads of mussel shells, fish bones and other debris of animals. When the river goes down, the shells and other articles disappear only to be succeeded by a fresh lot. This is evidence to those who have watched the coming and going of the strange things that they live upon such food.

It has been about four years since they were first noticed about Vevay. *The fisherman who saw the strange heads protruding from the stream had never heard of a mermaid, and his description was such as to cause the belief in the minds of the better educated that, after all, the old myth might be true in some degree.*

Some days since, Captain J. M. Ozler of Covington, [KY], who is in charge of a traveling art exhibit, came to this place to make arrangements for an entertainment. Her heard of the strange mermaid and paid their haunt several visits in the hope of being able to get a glimpse of them. In this he was successful, going so far as to get a pencil sketch of the male amphibian. Seated on the bank, he watched it swimming within 20 feet of the spot where he observed its movements.

From notes taken on the ground the description as furnished by Mr. Ozier states that the beast is about [five] feet in length and should weigh about 150 pounds. Its general color is yellowish. The body between the legs resemble that of a human being. Back of the hind legs it tapers to a point. This point in no way resembles a tail. The legs, four in number, resemble the arms and legs of the human. The fore legs are shorter than the hind pair and are used in the same manner as arms. The extremities resemble hands and are webbed and furnished with sharp claws. On the back and one-third of the way around the body appears a mass of straggling, coarse hair. The skin below the fore legs is thick and resembles elephant hide. On the arms and about the face and neck it is of a finer texture and brighter yellow color than the rest of the body.

The head of the nondescript beast is the most remarkable part of its makeup. It is devoid of hair and is strangely like that of a human being. Its ears are share pointed and stand up like those of a dog. There is no intelligence in the face … Mr. Ozier declares that it resembles to a great extent the freak known as Zip, or the What-is-it, which was exhibited first by P. T. Barnum. In swimming it seems to move without an effort and does not cause much commotion in the water. Only its head and a part of the slightly arched back are shown while swimming. When frightened, instead of diving like a duck or making a quick flop, the strange beast sinks from view like a stone. It is exceedingly timid in nature, fleeing at the first approach of a human being.

P. T. Barnum's "freak" mentioned in the article was similar to the Fiji mermaid, with the upper half of a juvenile monkey sewn to the lower half of a fish and then taxidermized to give the impression of a mermaid.

OHIO RIVER
OCTO-MAN

A n Ohio River cryptid known as "Octo-man" first appeared in the Cincinnati Post and Times-Star January 29, 1959 article, *What Is It?*, explaining:

Cincinnati, Clermont County and New Richmond police received telephone calls from men who said they saw "something come out of the river."

Officers at [the station] received calls from two different men. The first came from a man who said he saw the object about four miles from New Richmond. He said he could not describe the object.

The second caller with a different voice said he was a truck driver en route to Indianapolis. He said he was calling from a service station on Kellogg Avenue near the river bridge [Little Miami River] after passing through Mt. Washington toward Cincinnati.

"It came up out of the water", the truck driver said. "I can't describe it and I have never seen anything like it before. All I want to do is get out of here and get on to Indianapolis."

A dispatcher at [the station] said, "We didn't do anything after the first call. After the second one, we asked Hamilton County police if they had heard about it. We both sent cars out after [4:00 AM] and chased ghosts for a couple of hours, but we didn't find anything."

It really was a riot here. We kept waiting for someone to say, "Take me to your leader."

To add to the mystery, all the street lights along Kellogg Avenue from Lunken Airport to Coney Island went out about the same time. Police say the lights are on two different circuits, and that so far they have been unable to find why the lights went out.

Most dispatchers who received calls about the "monster" agree the callers sounded "shaken" but sober. They offer a number of theories of what the men might of seen.

Frank B. Heisler, A Clermont County dispatcher, believes the men might of seen a tree bobbing up and down in the water.

Cincinnati police for a time thought maybe someone had an auto accident, hit a pole, and rolled over in the mud. This would explain why the lights went out along Kellogg Ave. and what was seen coming up out of the water but they were unable to find any broken poles.

William Sprague, a lockman .... also thinks the men might of seen a tree drifting down stream.

Mr. Sprague said, "I've been on duty since midnight. I look out over the river a good deal of the time and I never saw a thing."

"The winds was strong all night and it whipped up waves six to eight feet high. That could fool a man. The wind tore a lot of driftwood loose too. I've been out on the river at night and the trees floating by in a dim light look spooky."

Maybe the "monster" was a tree.

The next day, the same newspaper ran the article, *Driver Swears It Happened*, where witnesses responded to the derogatory article:

Eye-witnesses still insist that an "indescribable" monster is bobbing around playfully in the Greater Cincinnati rivers and streams. A fellow who says he's a scientist working on things out of this world says he was driving across the Licking River Friday morning when "something leaped on the bridge."

"It was large, not a dog or a cat. It leaped in front of my car and on two legs and was taller than the auto. When I looked back in my mirror, it was moving along the bridge rail. "It was three or four times the size of a man and much bulkier. I have an eye and mind for dimensions and I know it was huge."

A young lady claims she spotted the thing in a creek near the Fort Thomas pumping station. It was like an octopus. It came up and then moved down.

An 11-year old phoned the Post and Times Star to ask if the green men really are coming out of the river in groups of 12 as his teacher said they were!

A woman pulled to the curb Saturday and yelled to a reporter: "We saw that thing this morning. Now you gonna put my name in the paper and call me a crack pot?"

Reported sightings of the "monster" at various points flowed in Friday to police of Cincinnati, New Richmond, Clermont and Hamilton Counties. Hamilton County officers spent two hours chasing ghosts along the Ohio and Little Miami Rivers. Street lights went out in parts of eastern Cincinnati about the same time adding to the eeriness. But the Cincinnati Gas and Electric Co. says it was a power failure caused by high winds.

Police said Saturday the phone calls have ended. The monster has left town. The Hamilton County dispatcher figures the people have quit drinking hair tonic. The man who'd like to believe in the monster's reality is Pepper Wilson, general manager of the Cincinnati Royals, who've had a less then sensational basketball season. "If that thing is over eight feet tall', we're interested."

The 1978 compiled book, *Big Foot*, added to the lore by documenting that on January 30, "a trucker driving on US Route 52" saw an "ugly" gray creature with tentacles crossing the road. Colin Bord's 1982 book, *The Bigfoot Casebook*, added that George Wagner, a trucker, had seen a "hulking creature" climb out of the river around the first week of February.

SKINWALKER

J. C. Johnson's YouTube videos, *Chief Dan Talks About Skin Walkers & The Furry Ones* and *Amelia & The Skinwalker*, explain that skinwalker, or yee naaldlooshii ("it goes on all fours"), is a Navajo legend that illustrates how black magic was believed to be used in the culture. These people are believed to be able to change their appearance to that of an animal. However, there's always something very peculiar about the appearance of the animal. The belief that these persons can change shapes isn't the most frightening aspect of these tales. Curses that the practitioners can place on people are what are most feared.

Misshapen or deformed animals, or those acting oddly, are interpreted as skinwalkers in this new mythology, having no connection to the Navajo people.

One of the more popular animals that alleged skinwalkers tend to imitate, according to lore, is coyotes. If they are spotted and the witness sees that they show signs of hair loss and "crusty" skin around the face, they could be interpreted as a skinwalker. In reality, such an animal is probably suffering from life-threatening mange.

SNALLYGASTER

Explored in Patrick Boyton's 2008 book, *Snallygaster*, tales of this monstrous mixture of bird and reptile began spreading throughout the Appalachian Mountains as newspaper reports of alleged encounters or sightings in Maryland began to be reprinted in other newspapers.

First appearing in South Mountain and Middletown Valley in Frederick County, where German immigrants called it Schneller Geist, meaning "quick ghost", its description evolved to include a metal beak lined with razor-like teeth, octopus tentacle-type tongue, "claws like steel hooks", and a single eye in the center of its forehead. Persons walking alone at night were said to be its victims, and some were said to have been found drained of their blood. Soon, hex signs displaying seven-pointed stars began being displayed on barns to prevent the creature from coming too close, which would be indicated if residents heard a strange train whistle-type sound.

TENNESSEE RIVER
MONSTER

Strikingly similar to the creature of Coosa River, the Tennessee River variety was documented in E. Randall Flyod's May 9, 1993 Herald-Journal article, *Sea serpent legend haunts Tennessee River*, where he documents the first sighting in 1822 by "a young Tennessee farmer named Buck Sutton" who was fishing "along a shaded area of the Tennessee River named Van's Hole" when he spotted a giant sea serpent-type creature in the water. The article goes on to say:

In 1827, Billy Burns was crossing the river near the same spot where Sutton had spotted the creature five years earlier. According to the version he later shared with friends, some kind of 'snake-like thing' charged his canoe, nearly causing him to capsize.

Burns said the creature – which he described as blue and yellow was at least as long as the canoe.

The next sighting was Jim Windom in 1829, who saw a "monstrous head" pop out of the water and observed the serpentine creature submerge, swim around, and that he "got a clear view of a tall, black din protruding two feet above the water", fitting with other accounts that Flyod summarized by writing:

Many of those who saw the monster described it as having a huge, dog-like head measuring two feet in length or more, flanked by a snake-like body at least 25 feet in length. According to most accounts, it had "frothing lips" and an ugly black fin that rose from the middle of a spiny back.

The article poses that the creature is an antemortem

apparition and that the "serpent's curse" either causes witnesses to pass away or that it appears to those who will soon pass away.

TENNESSEE TERROR

As outlined in Jennifer Watts' article, *Underwater Ghost Towns of Tennessee*, in the 1930s, the Tennessee Valley Authority (TVA) began construction on many dams throughout Tennessee to control flooding and provide electricity to its citizens. It seems that at many of these dams, 500-pound, giant catfish are swimming in the depths.

Fisherman stories usually follow the same motif, saying that they almost caught a fish that broke an incredibly strong line, or that the fish dragged the boat before the line snapped. Others may say that for whatever reason a diver was under the waves at a dam and saw a catfish "the size of a Volkswagen Beetle".

The tale is so popular that even Snopes did an article titled *Giant catfish* to discount it. In the entry, Barbara Mikkelson explains that to date, the largest catfish ever caught was "a 123-pound flathead catfish caught in Kansas".

THUNDERBIRD

A sacred symbol to many Indigenous cultures, it's been appropriated as a cryptid, a giant bird of prey appearing in Monsterquest's 2007 episode, *Birdzilla*. This new incarnation replaces the snallygaster folktale, or older concepts of dragons, as being a threat from above.

WAMPUS CAT

A *Topeka State Journal* article from April 4, 1914, defined it as a "cross between a mountain lion and a panther". In *The Des Moines Register* article from November 17, 1914, the reporter noted that community members regarded it as a "mythical cat-like being with a wicked disposition".

It seems that one of these big cats was captured, and was documented as displaying chimeric traits. According to a March 2, 1914 *Sterling Daily Standard* article, the reporter observed the creature in captivity and attempted to explain its history by saying that the term "wampus cat" originated in the black community which used it to scare children. The persons in the community said that with long claws and a nine-foot tail that could be used as a weapon, much like a kangaroo uses theirs.

However, this reporter seems to have watched one of these creatures. He writes that it was captured by two men who were out hunting in the Ouachita River Bottom Community. They spotted a black, cat-like creature, the size of a calf. Both men fired on the creature and returned to the community with it. The strange animal was displayed for three days, drawing a lot of attention.

The reporter who wrote the article went on to describe its unusual appearance as having the head and body of a cat, though it reminded him of a mixture between a bear and a hog, with long black fur with occasional white spots, small ears, a very long tail, and with eyes that resembled no animal that came to mind. He explained that the legs were short and stocky. The front paws reminded him of a burrowing badger, but the hind feet were cloven like a climbing goat.

After three days, the creature escaped, fleeing into history with more hidden oddities.

A *Drumright Weekly Derrick* newspaper article on August 1, 1925, outlined the very peculiar behavior of a large feline that frightened the residents of Drumright, Oklahoma so badly that they began considering outlawing jelly beans.

It was documented that the wampus cat entered the town by way of Tiger Creek while searching for a nest. It stole candy from children behind the gas station and was then caught tampering with a cash register when Mr. Drumright returned to his store from the bank.

The children's screams drew a crowd, and they scared the creature into jumping into a manhole to avoid being hit by bricks and stones.

A petition was circulating to collect signatures from concerned citizens. It was meant to stop the sale of jelly beans so that the creature wouldn't return to any stores to try to steal from children.

A *Sun Herald* newspaper article from February 1, 1927, documented another encounter in Electric Mills, Mississippi, which seemed to echo earlier sentiments that the creature was immune to injury. It explained that persons in the black community there had been losing chickens to it. Mrs. S. J. Smith lost 150 chickens to the creature. Bullets seemed to not affect it.

By 1939, with the publication of his book, *Fearsome Critters*, Henry H. Tryon had made the feline into a mythical animal of North American folklore. He wrote that it was venerated in black communities for catching deer-killing eagles.

He added fantastical elements to the feline, as well, writing that if it wades in a stream, the fish wouldn't bite for seven days, that its howl could curdle sourdough, that their footprints are only visible on solid rock, and that they liked to steal toothbrushes from prospectors.

In the 1952 book, *We Always Lie to Strangers*, it was incorrectly stated that the creature originated in the Ozark Mountains, and also added that it was an amphibious panther.

In *Demon in the Woods*, author Charles Edwin Price explains that a wampus cat is a bright-eyed, unusually large cat that walks on its hind legs. He writes that this creature has allegedly been sighted throughout the Tri-Cities, and documents an eyewitness sighting in Johnson City.

A man named W. H. told Price that his father was a carpenter who lived in Johnson City, and late one night, came face to face with one of these creatures. He explained that when the large cat-like creature reached Jones-Vance Pharmacy, it stood up and looked at him, and then walked away on its hind legs.

WENDIGO

Ojibwe teacher Basil Johnston described the being, not as claimed by fans of cryptids on the internet, in his 1996 book, *The Manitous*, saying:

> *The Wendigo was gaunt to the point of emaciation, its desiccated skin pulled tightly over its bones. With its bones pushing out against its skin, its complexion the ash-gray of death, and its eyes pushed back deep into their sockets, the Wendigo looked like a gaunt skeleton recently disinterred from the grave. What lips it had were tattered and bloody ... Unclean and suffering from suppuration of the flesh, the Wendigo gave off a strange and eerie odor of decay and decomposition, of death and corruption.*

One of the better resources on belief surrounding this spirit was found in Oji-Cree medicine man, Zhauwuno-geezhigo-gaubow, when in 1907, he and his brother performed exorcisms in Sandy Lake First Nation community in northern Ontario.

According to Shawn Smallman's 2015 book, *Dangerous Spirits*, the spirit was considered malicious and could possess people who violated social taboos and norms, causing them to become violent, greedy, and have an insatiable hunger, sometimes to the point of cannibalism even when other food was available. It was said to live in the coldest, most densely wooded forests, far away from people, and was most dangerous in wintertime.

Shawn goes on to write that seemingly possessed persons that the brothers felt they couldn't exorcise were murdered, and the medicine man was arrested, but he was able to escape and hanged himself before going to trial.

BIBLIOGRAPHY

"30-Foot Sea Serpent in Lake Erie." *The Indianapolis Times*, 17 July 1931.

Abingdon Democrat, 1857.

Alexandria Gazette & Daily Advertiser, 19 Sept. 1817.

"Another Beast On the Prowl?" *News and Observer*, 27 Apr. 1958.

Another Danger at Red River Gorge, www.uncoveror.com/flying.htm. Accessed 14 May 2024.

Asheville Citizen-Times, 15 Nov. 1987.

Bailey, Eric. "Bigfoot's Big Feat." *Los Angeles Times*, 19 Apr. 2003.

Barker, Gray. *The Silver Bridge: The Classic Mothman Tale*. Metadisc Books, 2008.

"Big Mongrel Dog Killed, Ending Scare Reports." *News and Record*, 17 Dec. 1954.

"Bigger than Saucers." *Los Angeles Herald*, 21 Aug. 1892.

Bingham, Emily. "Q&A: The Man behind Michigan's Dogman Legend." *MyNorth.Com*, 4 Sept. 2020, mynorth.com/2024/01/qa-the-man-behind-michigans-dogman-legend/.

Bord, Janet, and Colin Bord. *The Bigfoot Casebook*. Granada, 1982.

Boyton, Patrick, and R. M. Hanson. *Snallygaster: The Lost Legend of Frederick County*. 2008.

Burns, J. W. "Introducing B.C.'s Hairy Giants." *MacLean's Magazine*, 1 Apr. 1929.

Butler, William. *The Potter Enterprise*, 28 Apr. 1897.

Caledonian Mercury, 4 Dec. 1794.

"Capt. Woods Reports One of Terrible Aspect and Fiery Eyes." *The Evening World*, 16 July 1892.

The Charlotte Observer, 16 Dec. 1877.

Chicago Daily Tribune, 11 Oct. 1878.

Comstock, Jim F. *West Virginia Songbag*. J. Comstock, 1974.

Cook, Joedy. *Mothman Casebook*. Create Space Independent Publishing Platform, 2014.

Cougars in Tennessee, State of Tennessee, Wildlife Resources Agency, www.tn.gov/twra/wildlife/mammals/large/cougars.html. Accessed 14

May 2024.

Coyte, Kaye. "Creature of Catfish?" *The Kentucky Kernel*, 13 Feb. 1974.

Davis, Isabel, and Ted Bloecher. *Close Encounter at Kelly and Others of 1955.* Center for UFO Studies, 1978.

The Des Moines Register, 17 Nov. 1914.

"Driver Swears It Happened." *Cincinnati Post and Times-Star*, 30 Jan. 1959.

Drumright Weekly Derrick, 1 Aug. 1925.

Dudding, George. *Kentucky's Herrington Lake Monster*. GSD Publications, 2015.

Feschino, Frank C. *The Braxton County Monster: The Cover-up of the "Flatwoods Monster" Revealed*. Lulu Enterprises, 2013.

Flyod, E. Randall. "Sea Serpent Legend Haunts Tennessee River." *Herald-Journal*, 9 May 1993.

Forest and Stream, 1896.

The Gadsen Times, 6 June 1877.

Galloway, Brent Douglas. *Dictionary of Upriver Halkomelem*. University of California Press, 2009.

Gause, John. "Armed Hunting Party To Seek Bladenboro's 'Vampire Beast.'" *The Robesonian*, 5 Jan. 1954.

Godfrey, Linda S. *American Monsters: A History of Monster Lore, Legends, and Sightings in America*. Tarcher, 2014.

Godfrey, Linda S. *The Beast of Bray Road: Tailing Wisconsin's Werewolf*. 2015.

Hendersen, Frank. *Bigfoot in Georgia*. 2023.

The Highland Weekly News, 25 July 1861.

Holland, Jeffrey Scott, et al. *Weird Kentucky: Your Travel Guide to Kentucky's Local Legends and Best Kept Secrets*. Sterling Pub., 2008.

Houck, Tyler. *Cryptid U.S.* 2018.

The Ithaca Journal, 1 June 1929.

The Ithaca Journal, 17 Aug. 2007.

The Ithaca Journal, 5 Jan. 1897.

"Jay County's Fifty-Foot Snake." *The Indianapolis Journal*, 25 July 1891.

Johnson, J. C. "Amelia & the Skinwalker." *YouTube*, 18 Dec. 2010, youtu.be/wG5yRQCowwA?si=CpLT9INIpif8OrTf.

Johnson, J. C. "Chief Dan Talks about Skin Walkers & the Furry Ones." *YouTube*, 10 Dec. 2010, youtu.be/kWOQuf02J3w?si=DHvp_Feuv-Z3gZZ7.

Johnston, Basil. *The Manitous: The Spiritual World of the Ojibway*. Minnesota Historical Soc. Press, 2001.

Jorg Totsgi. "Big Hairy Indians Back of Ape Tale." *The Oregonian*, 15 July 1924.

The Journal of Spelean History, 2011.

Keel, John A. *The Mothman Prophecies*. Tor, 2013.

The Kentucky Lizardman, Kentucky Bigfoot Research Organization, www.kentuckybigfoot.com/cryptids. Accessed 14 May 2024.

"Lake Erie's Sea Serpent Seen." *Jamestown Weekly Alert*, 8 Nov. 1861.

"Lake Erie's Sea Serpent." *The Scranton Tribune*, 1861.

"The Legend of the Boojum." *Visit NC Smokies*, 10 Oct. 2023, visitncsmokies.com/blog/the-legend-of-the-boojum/.

MacDonald, Gregg. "The Legend of the Woodbooger." *Cooperative Living*, 1 Oct. 2022, www.co-opliving.com/4429/the-legend-of-the-woodbooger/.

Manget, Luke. "Wild Man of the Woods." *The Southern Highlander*, www.thesouthernhighlander.org/wild-man-of-the-woods. Accessed 14 May 2024.

Marshall, C. P. *The Cryptozoology of Cats*. 2024.

Mart, T. S., and Mel Cabre. *A Guide to Sky Monsters: Thunderbirds, the Jersey Devil, Mothman, and Other Flying Cryptids*. Red Lightning Books, 2023.

McCullough, Erin. "Haunted Legends: The Beast of the Land between the Lakes." *WKRN News 2*, 23 Oct. 2023, www.wkrn.com/special-reports/haunted-tennessee/haunted-legends-the-beast-of-the-land-between-the-lakes/.

McGlone, Ron. *Strange Creature Reported in Carmel Area*, Highland County Press, 19 Dec. 2014, highlandcountypress.com/news/strange-creature-reported-carmel-area#gsc.tab=0.

Mikkelson, Barbara. "Giant Catfish." *Snopes*, 31 Mar. 2015, www.snopes.com/fact-check/cat-o-nine-tales-2/.

Mikkelson, David. "15-Foot Eastern Diamondback Rattlesnake." *Snopes*, 8 July 2015, www.snopes.com/fact-check/15-foot-diamondback-rattler/.

"Mud Mermaids." *News and Citizen*, 18 Oct. 1894.

"Ohio Has a Sea Serpent Scare." *The Waterbury Democrat*, 21 July 1934.

Osborne, Clyde. "Bladen Beast Hunt Hampered." *The Charlotte Observer*, 7 Jan. 1954.

Pacunas, Beth, director. *Birdzilla. Monsterquest*, History, 21 Nov. 2007, Accessed 14 May 2024.

Perry, Douglas. "How a 1924 Bigfoot Battle on Mt. St. Helens Helped Launch a Legend." *The Oregonian*, 25 Jan. 2018.

Perry, San. *Jan's Tales*, www.guardiantales.com, 2002, web.archive.org/web/20090522204713/www.guardiantales.freewebspace.com/JANSTALES.html.

Price, Charles Edwin, and David Dixon. *Demon in the Woods: Tall Tales and True from East Tennessee.* Overmountain Press, 1992.

Ragland, Mike. "Monsters of the Coosa River." *Rome News-Tribune,* 21 May 2017.

Randolph, Vance, and Vance Randolph. *We Always Lie to Strangers.* 1949.

Rehn, Dana. *What Is the Meaning behind the Dog-Man Conjoined Twins in the Nuremberg Chronicle?,* 17 July 2022, danarehn.com/2021/10/03/what-is-the-meaning-behind-the-dog-man-conjoined-twins-in-the-nuremberg-chronicle/#:~:text=As%20described%20in%20the%20Nuremberg,of%20the%20dog%2Dheaded%20cynocephali.

"Sea Serpent Appears Again." *The Owosso Times,* 6 Aug. 1897.

"The Season Is Now Open." *Daily Tobacco Leaf-Chronicle,* 21 May 1892.

Shortridge, Bill J. *Lake Erie Sea Monster.* Createspace, 2021.

Sibray, David. "June 16 Marks Anniversary of Grafton Monster Sightings." *West Virginia Explorer,* 13 June 2023, wvexplorer.com/2018/06/13/june-16-anniversary-grafton-monster-sightings/.

"Slothfoot." *Cryptid Wiki,* Fandom, Inc., cryptidz.fandom.com/wiki/Slothfoot. Accessed 14 May 2024.

Smallman, Shawn C. *Dangerous Spirits: The Windigo in Myth and History.* Heritage House Publishing, 2015.

Statesman, Jan. 1829.

Statesville Record and Landmark, 29 Sept. 1995.

Sterling Daily Standard, 2 Mar. 1914.

Sucik, Nick. "Myth of Menace?" *The Advocate-Messenger,* 15 Mar. 2009.

Sucik, Nick. "Winged Snakes Seen throughout the U.S." *The Advocate-Messenger,* 22 Mar. 2009.

Sun Herald, 1 Feb. 1927.

Taylor, L. B. *Monsters of Virginia: Mysterious Creatures in the Old Dominion.* Stackpole Books, 2012.

The Times Leader, 26 Oct. 1973.

Topeka State Journal, 4 Apr. 1914.

Totsgi, Jorg. "Ape Hunt to Fail, Indians Predict." *The Oregonian,* 17 July 1924.

Tryon, Henry H. *Fearsome Critters.* The Idlewild Press, 1939.

Upshaw, Sarah E. "Herrington Lake 'Monster' Causes Quite a Ripple, Leaves Lake Residents Speculating." *The Advocate-Messenger,* 16 Feb. 1990.

"A Vanceburg Snake Story." *The Evening Bulletin,* 23 May 1899.

Ward, Joe. "'Monster' Reported Swimming in Herrington Lake." *The Courier-Journal,* 7 Aug. 1972.

Watts, Jennifer. "Underwater Ghost Towns of Tennessee." *Tennessee*

State Museum, tnmuseum.org/junior-curators/posts/underwater-ghost-towns-of-tennessee. Accessed 14 May 2024.

"What Is It?" *Cincinnati Post and Times-Star,* 29 Jan. 1959.

"The Wild Man of Ohio." *The Midland Journal,* 11 Mar. 1887.

"A Wild Man." *Chattanooga Daily Times,* 1 June 1890.

The Wilmington Morning Star, 15 Dec. 1877.

Winfield, Mason. "The Thirteen Creepies of the Western Door." *Buffalo Rising,* 31 Oct. 2015.

Yorgey, Cassandra. "Experts Deny Population of Cougars in Appalachian ..." *Exemplore,* 17 Feb. 2023, exemplore.com/news/anomalous-big-cats-appalachia.

"'blue Devil' Scare of 1939-1940." *Clio,* theclio.com/entry/85665. Accessed 14 May 2024.

"'Mystery Beast' Appears Again At Clifton Forge." *Covington Virginian,* 28 Oct. 1963.

Made in the USA
Columbia, SC
23 October 2024

e414e0fd-a726-4aad-af9f-fcb22cb082ecR01